AL WRIGHT

Minto

AL WRIGHT

Minto

SPIRIT MOUNTAIN PRESS

ISBN: 0-910871-13-2

Interviewing and Editing:
    Yvonne Yarber and Curt Madison

Material collected in Kona, Hawaii, March 1980,
    Fairbanks and Minto Flats, August 1982.

Manuscript approved by Al Wright February 1985
    in Kona, Hawaii.

**Library of Congress
Cataloging in Publication Data**

Madison, Curt
Yarber, Yvonne
        Wright, Al - Minto. A Biography
    YKSD Biography Series
    ISBN 0-910871-13-2

1. Wright, Al 2. Minto
3. Alaska Biography

SPIRIT MOUNTAIN PRESS
P.O. BOX 1214 FAIRBANKS, ALASKA 99707

Produced and Funded by:
    Yukon-Koyukuk School District of Alaska

Regional School Board:
    Luke Titus - Chairman
    Donald V. Honea - Vice Chairman
    Neil Morris - Secretary
    Patrick McCarty - Treasurer
    Eddie Bergman
    Cheryl DeHart
    Patrick Madros

Superintendent: Joe Cooper
Assistant Superintendent: Fred Lau
Project Coordinator: Don Kratzer

Supplemental funding:
    Johnson O'Malley Grant - EOOC14202516

Cover Photo:
    Al Wright in front of his plane on the beach of his Yukon River fish camp. Photo by Curt Madison.

Frontispiece:
    Aerial view of the Minto Flats looking west. Al Wright's pike fishing camp can be seen left center on the sharp bend of the Little Goldstream. Caches is on the other side of the bend. Minto Slough is the smaller body of water that meets the sharp bend of the Little Goldstream. Photo by Curt Madison 1982.

Acknowledgements

This book was made possible by the help of many people during the five years of its preparation. Al and Jeanne Wright were generous with their time and flew us to their camps at Minto Flats and the Yukon. Miranda Wright provided family tree information. Eliza Jones deciphered additional descendent data from Jesuit records. Bea Hagen typed the transcripts from hours of interviews with Al. Liza Vernet donated her time proofreading. Steve O'Brien clarified aviation terms. Bob Maguire invented this project. Joe Cooper, Fred Lau, and Mavis Brown took care of the administrative demands, and the Yukon-Koyukuk Regional School Board continue to support local curriculum. The people of Spirit Mountain Press: Larry Laraby, owner; Doug Miller, layout; and Eva Bee, typesetter, moved the manuscript to this finished book.

Foreword

This book is the twentieth produced by the Yukon-Koyukuk School District in a series meant to provide cultural understanding of our own area and relevant role models for students. Too often Interior Alaska is ignored in books or mentioned only in conjunction with its mineral resources such as the gold rush or oil pipeline. We are gauged by what we are worth to Outside people. People living in the Interior certainly have been affected by those things but also by missionaries, wage labor, fur prices, celebrations, spring hunts, schools, technology, potlatches, and much more. For residents, Interior Alaska is all of those things people do together, whether in the woods, on the river, in the village or on Two Street. It's a rich and varied culture often glossed over in favor of things more easily written and understood.

This project was begun in 1977 by Bob Maguire. Representatives of Indian Education Parent Committees from each of Yukon-Koyukuk School District's eleven villages met in Fairbanks February of 1978 to choose two people from each village to write about. A variety of selection means were used—from school committees to village council elections. Despite the fact that most of the representatives were women, few women were chosen for the books. As the years passed, more women were added to give a more complete accounting of recent cultural changes.

It is our goal to provide a vehicle for people who live around us so they can describe the events of their lives in their own words. To be singled out as an individual as we have done in this series has not always been comfortable for the biographees, particularly for those who carry the strong Koyukon value of being humble. Talking about oneself has been a conflict overridden by the desire and overwhelming need to give young people some understanding of their own history in a form they have become accustomed to. A growing number of elders who can't read or write themselves think young people won't believe anything unless it's written in a book. This project attempts to give oral knowledge equal time in the schools.

As materials of this kind become more common, methods of gathering and presenting oral history get better. The most important ingredient is trust. After many hours of interview, people often relax to the point of saying some personal things they prefer left unpublished. After editing the tape transcripts we bring the rough draft manuscript back to the biographees to let them add or delete things before it becomes public. Too often those of us living in rural Alaska have been researched *on* or written *about* for an audience far away. This series is meant to bring information full round--from us back to us for our own uses.

Too many people in the Interior have felt ripped-off by journalists and bureaucrats. Hundreds pass through every year, all wanting information and many never to return. Occasionally their finished work may find its way back to the source only to flare emotions when people feel misrepresented. Perhaps a tight deadline or the lack of travel money may be the excuse for not returning for verification or approval. That is no consolation for people who opened up and shared something of themselves and are left feeling betrayed. We work closely with the biographees to check facts and intentions. The books need to be intimate and daring but the last thing we want to do is make someone's life more difficult. We need to share information in a wholesome way. After all, we're all in this together.

Comments about the biographies, their use, corrections, questions, or anything else is welcome.

Curt Madison
Yvonne Yarber
December 10, 1982
Manley Hot Springs
Alaska 99756

Table Of Contents

Introduction

Al Wright has led a semi-nomadic life in the Athabaskan tradition, only his means are different. His father, son of an Athabaskan woman and a goldmine stampeder, was raised by the Episcopal Church. Arthur Wright accompanied Hudson Stuck and other early missionaries on their adventures. He married a mission nurse and was in charge of the Tanana Crossing mission when Al was born.

Since then Al has constantly been on the move. His construction and airplane business took him to every village in the Interior and beyond. Although he and his wife Jeanne are successful at business, subsistence foods are the cornerstone of their lives. Whether he is catching salmon and hunting moose in Alaska or growing avocadoes in Kona, Hawaii, he is getting his own food.

Many of Al's early years were spent in Minto and Nenana. He is a stockholder in the Minto village corporation. Because of his strong ties to the village, the Minto Indian Education Parent Committee chose him to be a part of this series.

Glossary

auger in — slang term to describe an airplane spinning or spiralling into the ground

Cat — Caterpillar Tractor Company bulldozer

Minto — The original village (Old Minto) prone to yearly flooding was located on the east bank of the Tanana River forty-four miles west of Fairbanks. It was relocated in 1970 on higher ground about twenty-five miles directly north of Old Minto. Minto is presently connected to Fairbanks by road.

Minto Flats — A large area of numerous lakes and streams also known as the Flats. The Tolovana River, Tatalina River, Washington Creek, Chatanika River and Goldstream River all feed into the Flats. The Minto Athabaskan people have traditionally used this area for fishing, hunting and other subsistence activities.

rat — muskrat

Tanana Crossing — Established as a telegraph station on the Fort Egbert (Eagle) - Valdez military telegraph line connecting the Yukon-Tanana uplands with Fort Gibbon (Tanana), constructed in 1902. The telegraph line crossed the Tanana River at this point resulting in the name Tanana Crossing. An Episcopal Mission was established in 1912. A post office named St. Timothys after the mission was put into service in 1920. The village name was changed to Tanacross in 1932 and the Post Office followed suit in 1934.

Tolovana — The Tolovana, located on the Tanana River near the mouth of the Tolovana River, was once a small village and telegraph station where Chief Alexander and his family lived.

Local Area

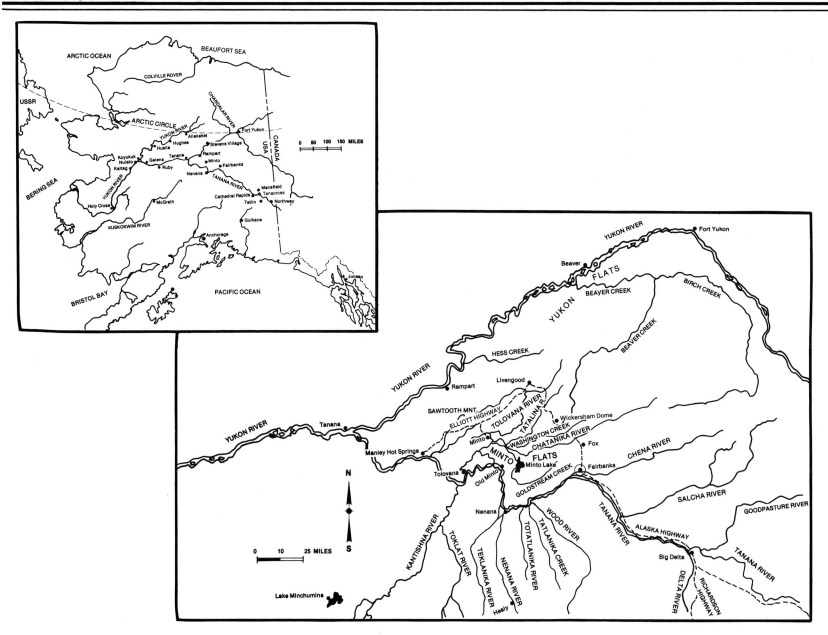

Chapter One: Growing Up

Missionary Parents

The only grandparent I knew was my grandmother Annie Glass in Minto. I was real small, only five, when we moved to Minto and I met her. Then I was seven when she died so I never got to know her very well. Dorothy Titus and Peter John told me stories about her. Apparently she grew up around Nulato someplace.

My grandfather came up in the gold rush from Montana. But he left the country when my dad was still a little kid so there aren't many stories about him. There's a little in the book *Sourdough Sagas* about his time around Rampart. Henry Wright was his name.

They say before he got to Alaska he was partners in a bar with some guy in Montana. The rush was on and he wanted to come up so he just tapped the cash register and came. Years later when he went back to say hello his partner pulled a gun out from under the counter and shot him. I just heard a few stories here and there and no one seems to know if they are true or not.

My dad never talked about him. Well, he didn't even know him, I guess. He was so small when his father left. After that the Episcopal Church took over raising my dad and he went to work following Bishop Rowe around the country. He ran dogs for the early time missionaries. In the summer he took them up and down the river by boat. Then he met my mother. They got

Annie Glass and Arthur Wright's half-sister Celia Wright near Ruby circa 1910. The Wright's had thought Annie Glass to be Arthur's mother but recent information backed by old Church records prove otherwise. See the family tree for additional information.

married and became missionaries themselves.

My dad got a pretty good education. He went to school in Tanana for awhile and then the Episcopal Church sent him Outside to Mt. Herman school in Massachusetts. He had a lot more education than I had that's for sure.

His name was Arthur Wright and my mother was Myrtle Wright. She was a nurse and probably one of the first ones ever in most of the villages we got to. She was doctor and the whole works to everybody.

She was in Nenana when the big flu hit there and a lot of people died off. Natives weren't immune to the flu bug like the White people were so more of them died. Just small diseases were bad in those days. Kids, anybody, would die from measles because they didn't have any immunity.

I was born in Tanana Crossing, April 26, 1925. Another missionary nurse came up by dog team from Nenana to stay with my mother just before I was born. We lived in Tanana Crossing about a year after that. Then we moved to Nenana.

In 1925 there were no roads into Tanana Crossing. Only way you could get there was by boat. There was a privately owned wood-burning sternwheel steamboat they ran from Big Delta upriver. They'd take off and head up till they ran out of fuel. Then all the crew and passengers would cut enough wood for another couple days and take off again. When they got to places like Cathedral Bluffs where the river was swift the boat didn't have enough poop to push it, so everyone would have to get out and haul the boat through with a rope. It took two weeks to get from Big Delta to Tanana Crossing.

About forty or fifty people were living there, but several villages, like Mansfield and Tetlin, were close by. Tanana

Newborn Al Wright held by his father Arthur, brother Gene standing next to their mother Myrtle Wright. Tanana Crossing 1925.

Al, Arthur and Gene Wright visiting Fairbanks from Tanana Crossing, 1926.

Crossing was just a central place. It started as a trading post because everyone came down to the Tanana River in the summer to do their fishing. Then the mission started and it grew a little. I remember my dad talking about going to other villages nearby to have weddings and church services and stuff.

My mother was practicing her nursing all the time. One time some guys were out hunting and one of them got shot, blew his jaw out. When they brought him back in they said there was no way he was going to live. The medicine men worked on him, but they were just getting him ready to die. So she went to work patching him up and made him live. I guess they figured she might be a pretty good medicine woman.

There were some conflicts and they probably resented her doing this nursing thing because it's altogether different than their way of tending to their problems. No real serious conflicts, though, because she never pushed them. She knew that if she were out to get a medicine man, he'd be out to get her, too. She got along pretty good with everybody.

Later they moved the village to the south side of the river

"I don't know who that woman is but that's me next to her and Gene on the right. We're going to Big Delta on the boat that ran from Tanana Crossing. From Big Delta we went on to Fairbanks. Circa 1927.

Al's mother, Myrtle at her Fairbanks home April 21, 1957. The moose skin painting behind her was done by Erika Neilsen.

Al and Gene Wright at Tanana Crossing 1927, the year before the family moved.

"That's the whole tribe in that canoe during the flood in Nenana around 1928 or '29. Gene in the back with the pilot hat, my dad, my mother holding Don, then Gareth and me in front with the stick."

"Jesus Christ, what an outfit. Me, Gareth and Gene at Nenana just before we went to Minto."

The same flood at Nenana. L-r: brothers Al, Gene, Gareth and Don Wright in a Peterborough canoe.

14

and changed the name to Tanacross. The army built an emergency airstrip there to ferry planes over to Russia during World War II. The strip is still there and I use it occasionally but I've never lived there again. From there we went to Nenana for four years and then to Minto.

Old Minto

My dad's mother, Annie Glass, was living in Minto so we moved there in 1930. That's why I'm a member of the Minto village corporation now. I was just old enough to start hunting before we left. My dad bought me a single shot .22 and I'd go out for ducks and muskrats in the ponds close around. They were always chasing me down because they thought I would get lost or hurt or something. But I always liked to hunt.

"That's at Tanana Crossing too, the mission church in the background. My mom, me and Gene with some of those dogs we had such a problem with. They were a quarter wolf and liked nothing better than to fight. They'd tear each other to shreds. You'd have to take a 2 X 4 and knock them cold before they'd quit fighting. We used them in Nenana for hauling wood and whatever we had to do." 1927.

Dad showed us how to get by in the woods. We'd go out and live in camp in the wintertime when it was cold. He took us hunting and fishing all the time so we knew how to do things right from when we were pretty small. We never used a tent. Just siwashed it under spruce boughs or something.

The church gave him some money but it wasn't enough to live on so we always had a big garden in the summer. Every summer we had a fish wheel for salmon and set nets in the spring for whitefish and pike. We probably lived half off the country and half off what we got from the church for a living.

One trip I'll never forget, my dad took me about ten miles upstream from Minto to a slough called Totchaket. Springtime we were fishing for pike with nets. He pulled a net full of pike out and told me not to put my finger in their mouth or I'd get bit.

So, naturally, the first thing I did was go down to the boat when he went up to make camp and stick my finger in one pike's mouth to feel his teeth. He clamped down on me and I started screaming and hollering. Dad had to come down to pry open the mouth to get my finger out.

Spring and fall we would always hunt caribou. They came through by the thousands. For ten days straight just a steady stream from one side to the other. After 1948 I didn't see any more come through. There are lots of theories why.

Game population gets high then declines and starts over again in cycles. For those caribou, the wolf population got high and diseases cut them down. Then of course, it's the same bunch of caribou that cross the Steese Highway all the time. In later years between the wolves and the people, they about annihilated them. Hunters drove out from Fairbanks and killed bulls and cows alike. The Kantishna herd stopped joining up with the Porcupine.

When I first got to Minto it was all dirt paths and one room cabins. They didn't build the boardwalk until sometime in the sixties. Nearly every spring Minto got flooded out by the Tanana River. My dad built a two-story log house for the mission. Most all the original village from those days is in the river now. It all caved in so the

"That was our house at Minto, the mission house. My dad, a guy named John Hill, and Moses Crookshank from Beaver built it. It's caved in the river now. It was a nice house. Old John Hill was a Finn and a really good carpenter. He had a sawmill set up across the river they cut the lumber with. Then they cut lumber for all the other houses around Old Minto. Must be around 1930."

people moved farther back. Dragged their cabins or built new ones. But then most people didn't live in the village year-round. They'd go out to their traplines all winter.

My dad tried to start a school but he had a real hard time because there weren't enough kids around. They'd be there for a little while then they'd all be gone. Each kid would have to bring a stick of wood to school in the morning for tuition. If they had enough wood for the stove to last through the day they'd keep going. He'd run the school for a month or so then most of them would take off with their families to their traplines, and he'd close it down.

The Minto mission was mainly a church. They had services on Sunday and my mother took care of all the nursing problems. Outside church people would send clothes and all that kind of stuff up and my dad would distribute it out to the people that needed it. They did whatever missionaries do and we lived in Minto year-round.

Sometimes it got pretty quiet when we were the only ones there. Springtime, people all went out to the rat camps. They'd go before breakup and wouldn't come back until after the ice was gone. It's about fifteen miles back on the lakes by dog team. Then to come out they'd have to go sixty miles down the Chatanika River into the Tolovana, down the Tolovana to the Tanana, then upstream to the village.

As soon as the salmon started running they'd move back out to their fish camps. Each family or couple families would have a camp along the Tanana River where they kept their wheel. Finally at freeze-up they put their wheels away and moved back to the village again. Most of the people didn't stay in Minto permanently until the BIA built a school and the government passed a law requiring all the kids to go to school. After that the men went trapping alone so the wives and kids could stay home.

My dad made a few trips out to the camps before breakup for services or funerals, but usually we just have to stay in the village and take care of the place. He could talk the Native language as well as anyone so he did a lot of translating. He could communicate with the old people real good.

The Whiteman way of doing things was just getting started then, but they did use coffins for burial. Before they used birch bark. I know because one time some archeologist came along and wanted to dig up old bones of people. I went along with my dad when he showed him some graves. He dug them up and we could see how they were all wrapped up in birch bark.

Traders On The River

Everybody curses the traders, saying what bad people they were. But I don't think they were like that. They made money, yeah, they made a lot of money, but they helped those people, too. Say there were twenty or thirty families living in a village. The trader would be supplying all the needs they have for food and clothing and stuff. The people go to work trapping and bring their fur in to him. He gives them a certain price for it and they pay up their bill that they charged at the store until they got their fur. They pay it all up and they have a few extra dollars to spend on booze or whatever they want. Then they're broke again. They paid up last year's bill, had their drunk and they're broke with nothing to eat. So the trader gives them food on credit again. Everything the man needs to keep his family going for the year. Next year he pays him off and they do the same thing again. So, you know, he's seeing that the family made a living through the year. Each one.

Then most of the time he'd take one guy and make an example of him. Someone would say the trader wasn't paying enough for fur. That guy would take his fur down to another buyer. Then he'd blow all his money without paying his store bill. The trader would say, "Okay, no more credit. I'm going to cut you off."

The guy would have such a tough time making a living that the rest of the

John Vachon the trader at Tolovana after a rabbit hunt, late fall 1913.

people would see this and not want to get in the same position. That way they wouldn't go sell their fur someplace else because they were dependent on the trader for a living.

See, all the kids would get something to eat through the year regardless of what happened because the trader would be carrying them. 'Course a lot of traders would nick the people good for their fur and make a lot of money on it. But to me it didn't make any difference. I feel that if he didn't get it then it was going to be blown on booze anyway. So why was he so bad?

Dominic Vernetti lived in Koyukuk. He was probably the most successful trader in the Interior. He took care of all the people up the Koyukuk and on the middle Yukon. And they took care of him. The way he sold liquor, he had his liquor store open for one hour. He'd ration out the booze. After that hour no matter how these guys tried he wouldn't give them any more until a certain time. He took all their money, sure, but he took care of them. They all made out.

I'll never forget one story. A guy bought a twelve-horse inboard motor from Dominic. He said he'd pay something each year for it until it's paid off. So he's paying each year and the amount the engine was worth it should have been paid off in three or four years. After about ten years somebody asked him, "Gee, you ought to have your motor about paid off by now don't you think?"

"Well, I don't know, might be," he said.

He went up to Dominic and asked him about it. Dominic tells him, "Yeah, this was the last payment. It's all yours now."

I knew Dominic real well because I used to run a flying operation out of Koyukuk for three years. He was the banker and everything. He paid all the charters for everybody. We'd fly those people to all their traplines and he'd pay the bills. Then he'd collect it from them when they brought their fur in. And nobody could put anything over on him.

I remember once we went into this camp in December, about the middle of the marten season. He was going around gathering up skins. Taking a few things around and visiting people. He used to do that once in awhile. He'd make sure he'd visit the people that really owed him a lot of money, you know. We went in one tent and the guy brought his fur out. Laid it all down. They haggled about the price for awhile then Dominic bought the fur from him. Here it was all second grade stuff so he looked around and said, "Where's the rest of your fur?"

"That's all. There's no more," he says.

Dominic walks over, reaches under a mattress and pulls out a whole string of first-class prime marten. They guy just laughed and said, "Well, I tried anyway." Dominic graded out the skins and put them on account. It was pretty hard to pull anything over on him.

Towards spring, sometime in March, was Dominic's birthday. He'd have a big party and nearly everybody from the villages around there would come. He furnished everything, turkeys, crackers, spaghetti. The people supplied

Al and Jeanne Wright Collection

Episcopal Diocese Collection

L-r: Al, Gareth, and Gene Wright making ice cream in Nenana with Dixie Hall's boys Robert and Barbi. Al pounding ice with an ax. Circa 1934.

The old mission at Nenana on the left which has since fallen in the river. The bridge over the Tanana River at Nenana in the background.

meat and fish and all the women would get together to do the cooking.

That was really the time to make some money. We'd fly in nearly everybody from Nulato, Kaltag, Galena, Huslia, and Allakaket. It was a big event with dog races and everything.

Every village had a trader. Plus there were some other people scattered along the river. The mouth of the Tolovana River was a good place for a store because people coming down the Tolovana stopped there as well as the people coming out the Kantishna. They did pretty good until airplanes came in and people took their furs into Nenana or Fairbanks. All the traders operated basically the same way except some of them were a lot shrewder than others.

L-r back: Gareth and Al Wright with their brothers Jules and Forrest ("Punk") in front. Nenana 1943.

Nenana

When I was about nine we left Minto and moved to Nenana. My dad worked mostly in the shipyard where they built the steamer *Nenana*. In the winter we cut wood. That was our job after school or on Saturdays and Sundays. We'd go help the old man cut wood or haul a load of coal. We had a Model-T truck for making deliveries in town. It cost us fifty dollars and took us about six months to pay for it. We cut sixteen-foot wood into sixteen-inch lengths for a dollar and a half a cord. Or we went out into the woods and hauled a cord into town for eight dollars landed. We used a Sears and Roebuck wood saw on a sled dragged around by the truck. At first we didn't have a motor for it so we just jacked up the truck and ran it with a belt from the back wheel.

Years ago there weren't as many people fishing, but there were more fish taken. There were no snow machines so everybody had dog teams and fed their dogs fish. When I first started flying I used to fly a lot of fish out of Koyukuk and down the lower Yukon.

Like I said, Dominic Vernetti was the trader at Koyukuk. He had a boat and in the summer he'd go up the Yukon river to each fish camp and buy all their fish. He'd go up as far as Ruby and down to Kaltag to buy tons and tons of fish dried and baled for dog feed. He carried stuff on his boat to trade for the fish. Groceries and clothes and what have you from the store. He took the fish back to his big warehouse in Koyukuk. Then in the winter he'd sell it back to the fishermen when they went trapping. It was good for them because they could make their living through the year. And it was good for Dominic because he'd buy it for five cents a pound and sell it for ten cents back to them. Everybody had dogs and they all had to have dried fish. People on the lower Tanana sold fish at Tolovana, Nenana and at Minto when Johnny Campbell was there.

When I was a kid in Nenana we used to cut three or four hundred fish a day for maybe two months. Bundle them and bale them for five cents a pound dried. That meant you were getting five cents a fish after you processed it. One pound per fish after cutting the backbone out, scoring them, hanging them, drying them, putting them in the baler and packing them into fifty pound bundles. All along the river each family would have a fish camp and they'd do the same thing.

We had our camp on the island across from Nenana where the highway bridge goes now. My dad would come over and build a wheel and get us all set up. Then mostly us kids would go over there and do all the fishing while he was working in the shipyard. Of course, my mother was taking care of all the little kids. Being the nurse around town, she was busy all the time. So any of us who were old enough to hold a knife would go over there and cut fish. I started when I was about nine years old. We just lived over there in the summer.

I had gone to kindergarten in Nenana, then when we went to Minto there was no more school. We didn't go to school for three years. When I came back they put me in the second or third grade, but I was already behind.

When I got to the sixth grade we had a teacher who could care less whether we learned anything or not. My mother didn't know it but we used to jump out the window and play hooky all day. This teacher never said anything and we never learned anything. By the time I got to the eighth grade I figured this schooling was a waste of time. There were better things to do so I just quit and went about my business. It was a mistake, but I did it. Hauling wood, working, earning money any way I could.

I think I was about fifteen when I started working on construction jobs. I told them I knew all about equipment. I really didn't know anything, but I thought it was a good way to learn.

The first time I was on a Road Commission job, I had never been on a Cat before in my life. I wanted to run one in the worst way. I told them I knew how. The Cat was broke down so the superintendent took me to where the mechanic was fixing it about five miles from camp. Lucky he left it running because I didn't even know how to start it. They told me to walk it back and they all left. I finally figured out how to put it in gear and took off down the road. As I went along I experimented with this and that to find out what went where and why. They knew I didn't know anything but they had to go along with me because they couldn't get anyone else.

The Second World War started right about then and they wiped everyone out of the country that could go to war. That just left a bunch of old men and kids to do all the work. In 1942 when I was seventeen, I went to Bettles to help build the communication site. They were giving these planes to Russia and needed a beacon. After that I worked on the airports at Nenana,

Al just before leaving for the army, 1944.

Al Wright leaving for the army. His mother, Myrtle seeing him off at the train in Nenana, 1944.

Al and Jeanne Wright Collection

Al and Jeanne Wright Collection

23

Summit, and Gulkana and the Richardson Highway to Anchorage. There's a funny story with that one. But it doesn't sound funny until the end.

Another guy on the crew and I liked to fish for grayling. He salted them down for the winter. After work we'd go up the stream and catch a bunch of fish. One day I was supposed to meet him at a certain spot on the creek and some way we missed each other. So I'm staying around there fishing, waiting for him. He went back to the camp, had his supper, and came looking for me. There were a lot of bears around and he figured one had me up a tree.

He came with a couple of other guys and brought along his .30-'06. He walked right up to where I was fishing. We talked for awhile and I said I had a string of fish around the bend. I told him I'd pick them up then meet him back there and go to camp. I pulled my bamboo fishing pole into three pieces, you know how they come apart, and bent down to go through the thick brush. I'm going along and all of a sudden I saw a big flash. Next thing I know I'm on my hand and knees, blood running out all over. It felt like the whole back of my head was blown out. I thought this guy shot me with his .30-'06 so I was feeling for a big hole in the back of my head. It wasn't there.

Finally I look up and there's a guy with a shotgun. "I didn't mean to kill you! I didn't mean to kill you!" he kept saying. He was a kid working in the same camp who had come up to look for me. When he saw me coming through the brush he thought I was a bear and shot me. He'd have killed me but he missed. I just caught the side of the shot. It knocked some teeth out and some lead went through my nose. My shoulder was filled with shot. It knocked me out colder than a mackeral. You know how a rabbit kicks when he's shot? I did the same thing. Just tore everything up.

Well, I hollered up at these other guys, "I'm shot!" But apparently this guy with the .30-'06 had shot at a stump in the creek the same instant this other guy let off the shotgun and they didn't hear it. They thought I was kidding. Finally they came along, gathered me up and whipped me out to the road. I was in the hospital for the next couple of weeks while they picked shot out.

Two weeks later a Fish and Game officer came around. They had heard about this incident. At that time there were seasons on bears. You couldn't hunt them all summer so they nabbed this kid. Caught him and fined him fifty dollars for hunting bears out of season. Shooting me didn't count. I read about it in the *Alaska Sportsman* a year or so later.

Chapter Two: Airplane Business

Learn To Fly

All the time working construction, I was trying to get in the army. They wouldn't let me in because I was getting deferments to run this equipment around. It was supposed to be defense stuff we were building, but finally I just quit. Then they drafted me right off the bat.

The army put me in the infantry, and wouldn't let me operate anything. When I got out of the army, I went back to running equipment. Not long later I found out you could learn how to fly under this G.I. Bill. I snapped that right up. I was only going to do it for my own use, piddling around, but I never got away from it.

I was working in a coal mine at Healy during my lessons. I saved my money until I had enough to buy an airplane, a 65-Taylorcraft, and started gypoing around. One day I was sitting out at the field with nothing to do and a guy came along needing a charter. It was in the spring and he had some furs up on the Ladue River he wanted to pick up. I had no idea where that was, but I said sure. Turns out it was way over on the Alaska/Canada border. We had to stop in Northway to refuel. It was the longest trip I'd ever made in my life. I thought it was to the end of nowhere. It took two loads to get the furs out in my little T-craft. When he paid me off for the trip I thought "Boy, this is the way to make some money."

From then I started hauling trappers here and there. It just kind of developed into a business. When I'd be too broke I'd go to work for awhile

Al Wright just out of boot camp with brother "Punk". 1944.

26

then go back to flying. That first airplane chartered out for twenty dollars an hour, fuel, pilot, and everything. No one was flying into Minto, so I started going there, too.

The army gave veterans bidding preference at surplus auctions and I got a new pair of floats for the plane for six hundred dollars. That spring, the first time I was putting the floats on at the field in Fairbanks, a guy working for Wien's came up to me.

"When are you going to be finished putting this plane on floats?" he asked me. It was still before the ice went out of the river.

"Well, I just about have it. What's the matter?"

"There's a guy down on a lake," he said, "and he's dying. We went down to pick him up with the Seabee but we couldn't land because there's ice along the edge and the wing float wouldn't clear it. We can't get in there. We wondered if you could do it."

"It will take me a couple hours to finish here, but as soon as I can, I'll go get him."

It was Matthew and Robert Titus' brother. He was real sick around Six Mile Lake in the Minto Flats. I finished the airplane and dumped it in the water. I had never flown floats before in my life. I took off and picked this guy up and brought him back. After that I flew about two hundred hours on floats before I got my legal rating. All summer I went everywhere.

Finally the Feds caught up with me and I had to get a license. I never had any instruction. I just picked it up and learned myself. It was no problem passing the rating exam. But I've always had a tough time getting ratings and licenses because I never had very much education. I went to the eighth grade but three or four of those years I never learned a damn thing. They had some teachers that could care less if you learned. So I preferred not to learn. I never learned how to read well or write or spell. All through my life I had a tough time on account of that.

27

Crash And Burn

After a few years with the little T-craft I bought a gull-wing Stinson. I was flying around a lot and doing pretty good with it. Along towards fall I took it into the shop to have some work done and had to spend everything I made fixing it up. Everything was fixed except for a selector valve in the floor between the pilot and co-pilot seats where you switch fuel tanks. It had been leaking for over a year and it never bothered me. I couldn't get a new one. It had to be ordered.

Anyway I had a load of building material, lumber and stuff, and a passenger Hank Olsen to haul down from Fairbanks to Nenana. Middle of November and it was pretty cold. We had heavy parkas on. By the time we got to Nenana it was getting dark already. I circled around to attract a ride in from the airfield. Just as I started my turn I saw a big flash. Hank yells out, "Jeez, we're on fire!"

The whole back of the airplane was on fire. He grabbed the fire extinguisher, but it was absolutely useless on that much fire. We were at five hundred feet right over town. Hank opened the door and I thought he was going to jump out. "Don't jump," I said. "Just unhook your belt. I'll try to get to the runway. If we touch the runway, jump out and I'll be right behind you. We'll let the airplane go. That'll be our only chance to survive."

Then the flames really came in. Hank grabbed my Woods sleeping bag and wrapped himself up in it. I pulled my parka hood up and had mitts on trying to fly the airplane. The flames were really rolling around so I couldn't see out the window anymore. I just tried to watch the instruments to keep the airplane level. That last thing I saw on the instruments was three hundred feet of altitude at a hundred and thirty

"The same plane in the picture on the Chena. Same one I put in the trees, too. This one is on Beaver Creek 1949. I look so scroungy because I was forced down when one of my tanks sprung a leak and I lost my gasoline. I had a fur buyer with me and wasn't on a flight plan so nobody knew where we were. We sat there for three days until somebody happened to fly by and see us. It was cold, about thirty or forty below. We were lucky there was an old trapper cabin there I didn't even know about. I always carried a survival kit, enough groceries to last a couple weeks."

"That's the same plane I have in the picture at Beaver Creek but I didn't have the sign on the side. I used to keep the airplane there on the Chena River near the Cushman Street Bridge. I used to take off under the bridge and around the bend. The picture was made into a postcard. It was spring when the ice was going out and I stretched logs across the front to protect the floats." Circa 1948.

miles an hour. Then it exploded.

I figured, hell, this is it. We're dead. There's no way we're going to get out of this one. So I just sat there, you know, and pulled the stick all the way back. I shut the engine off and I could feel the airplane quit flying. We fell. When we hit the trees one wing was pulled off and we slid sideways down. The landing gear ripped off. Finally we came to a stop. With all this going on I didn't know what was happening. Fire was every place. I felt my hands were on the windshield so I tried to break it out, but I couldn't.

The way the seats were in that airplane you had to go back between them to get to the door. I whipped around headed for the door. I figured I wasn't even going to feel for it. I'd just ram my shoulder against it and push out. There was no door there! I sprawled out right on the ground!

I hollered for Hank, but didn't get any answer. So I reached in feeling around. I touched his hand and grabbed him out. He was all tangled up in the sleeping bag but still conscious. I got him out and started running away. About thirty feet off, my legs just went out from under me. I passed out colder than a turkey. I had inhaled so much fumes and smoke it finally got me. If I had passed out inside the plane, we both would have burned up.

Apparently I had slid my face up the instrument panel and cut my nose off. The cut went right up around my eye and opened up my scalp. The other eye was cut under the lid and the lid was pulled up so I couldn't see anything. After I came to I thought, "Oh Christ, I'm blind!"

My youngest brother and another guy dragged us out to the road. I had turned the plane and lined up with the runway just about a hundred feet short of it. The plane was really burning. The fire department showed up and tried to put it out. They thought we were still in it.

The fabric on those planes was covered with nitrate dope. It's just like powder. Once it gets started, it goes. People watching from the ground said it was like seeing a comet. Gradually they could see the airplane frame take form as the skin burned off and we fell. But we had that tail-heavy load and we fell real flat. That's what saved us.

There happened to be a doctor in Nenana removing tonsils and adenoids from the mission kids. Doctor Dick. He's an eye, ear, nose, and throat specialist in Anchorage now. They carted me up to him and he went to work sewing me back together. He did a good job. There's hardly a scar that shows now.

We couldn't either one of us move for over a week. It was like somebody took a sledge hammer and worked every bone in my body over. Smashed it. We didn't have any broken bones but we were just beat up from hitting so hard.

It was getting towards Christmas and things were really tough. I was broke, didn't have nothing. I had a wife and kid to take care of. My youngest brother was living with me then, too. One eye was all bandaged up yet, but I could see out of the other one. I figured I had to get back to work. Do something. Then this fur buyer, Goldberg, came along. He wanted to go down to Tolovana to buy some fur. The trip cost fifteen dollars. It was fifty below.

I never flew that little plane, the T-craft, in that temperature before. But I figured I was in such bad shape financially I'd better take the trip. I fire-potted the airplane, got it warmed up good and hot, loaded up and took off. We just got off the end of the runway and the engine quit. I wrecked within two hundred feet of where I crashed the gull-wing. Once it got in that cold air the gas wouldn't evaporate and the engine wouldn't run.

I was wiped out. I was out of airplanes and out of money. Out of everything. When I finally healed up nobody wanted to give me credit to buy a new plane, because I was such a poor risk. I had to rent an airplane.

Not long after that a good friend of mine, Hans Ratzebeck came along. He had a flying business down the Yukon River and had gone through a similiar ordeal with a couple airplanes. He was broke, too, so we were crying on each other's shoulder about our bad fortunes. We decided to go into business together. We really went gung-ho with a new operation. Everything clicked right. Within three years we owned nine airplanes and had every private pilot in the country flying for us.

A lot of things were going around 1950. People wanted to fly and we had better airplanes. There was no road between Fairbanks and Nenana so we had a lot of traffic there. We went to Minto and had a run all the way downriver to Kaltag. We based one plane in Koyukuk, but we had to fly fuel down to it from Nenana to keep it going through the winter. The barges didn't bring enough fuel down there in the summer. We had another gull-wing then and I'd fly three barrels and three cans down to Koyukuk. I'd leave the barrels and put the cans into the gull-wing to get back. Then I kept weaning it down. I'd leave one can, then another, in Koyukuk. Until I came in on a whisker. A couple times I ran out of gas on the runway after landing. Trying to cut it that close. It cost so much to haul gas all the way to Koyukuk, I tried to leave as much there as I could.

Maintenance is one of the key things to keep a flying business going. Mostly it's money. If you don't have the money to do the maintenance, you don't do it. But the thing is if you don't keep the airplanes up, you won't be in business long anyway. And if you can't keep them up you shouldn't be in business. I always went as strong on maintenance as I could. We had a good record.

Wolf Control

The Minto Flats was always a rich area. There used to be a lot of moose in there, but they got chomped down. They're starting to come back now, but they got hunted heavy in the late sixties and early seventies. The hunters and the wolves really took a toll. See,

Al flying towards Hess Creek on the Yukon River 1982.

we had a big increase in wolves in that country. It goes back to the government programs in the fifties.

There were so many wolves that this game in the flats was going down all over the state. The government hired a bunch of crews to drop poison bait all over the Alaska Range, the Brooks Range, and the whole valley. They killed thousands and thousands of wolves. But the word got out that not only wolves but bears, foxes, wolverines, and birds ate the bait. They died, too. But that's probably what saved the game in Alaska. The rest of this stuff came back pretty fast and the game started building up. In the late sixties we had a peak population of game. You could go get a moose any time you wanted it. Then they took the bounty off the wolves and started protecting them. The game population plummeted.

"I was flying for people on the 'Fishwheel Gold Strike' on the Yukon River around 1948, about two years after I started flying. That's a funny story..."

There were bad weather conditions and heavy hunting pressure, but in areas that weren't hunted the game went, too. Completely went. The country was flat overrun with wolves again.

If the government had left the bounty on and controlled the wolves we'd been alright. But they didn't so it all went to pot. Now they started in on some pilot projects of controlling wolves and the game is coming back in those areas. But if they kept control of the thing right from the start we'd still be in good shape for game. I know, I was hunting wolves in the fifties. We took over three thousand wolves north of the Brooks Range by airplane in one month. It hardly dented the population.

Around 1970 a bunch of wolves moved into the Minto Flats. I killed about ten or fifteen of them. I was always preaching to control the wolves, but the pressure Fish and Game was getting from the environmentalists and everybody they couldn't kill them anymore. I did a lot of flying for Fish and Game surveys. All kinds from counting fish to wolves and moose and

32

caribou. I decided to run a little survey on my own.

I was flying into Minto quite a bit from Fairbanks so once a week I flew down the Chatanika River from where the bridge crosses it on the Steese to the Flats. I really counted good and I saw twelve moose in that one ten mile area. I knew a pack of wolves was working that same place so I watched them. They got about a moose a week. I started in November and by the end of January there wasn't one moose left. Eight wolves in that pack and they were really smart. As soon as they heard an airplane they'd head for cover. I killed one, but you have to get them in the open.

They want to control just one side. If they'd control everything they could sustain a nice even flow of animals. It would be good for everybody. You can't eat a wolf or a bear, I don't anyway. They kill off so many moose and caribou you wouldn't believe it. Fish and Game is just starting to see that. I've lived in the woods so long and flown over so much of the country that I can see what's going on. But try to convince somebody. It's impossible. You got to show them the actual act before they'll believe you and it's hard to do that. You come on one of these drastic instances once in a year where you can see exactly what's going on. Most of the stuff happens at night.

I've seen bears kill a moose. They kill them so easy. That's one of the things that declined the caribou herds. Bears get in a calving area and kill those calves when they were born. Just grab them, kill them, eat them if they felt like it, and let them go if they didn't.

Wolves, too. They get in a calving area and let the pups practice. Pups kill the calves because they can get them easy. And they just eat what they want. I think this business about only

"I was wolf hunting on the North Slope, 1959. That's when they had a fifty dollar bounty and you could get another fifty bucks for the skin. Lucky to make your gasoline money flying all over the place to find them. I'd hang the wolf on the struts and skin it out."

33

getting the sick and wounded is flat baloney all the way down the line. A wolf won't kill a sick caribou and eat him. He'll go get the biggest, fattest one he can find just like a man will. If he'd got nothing else, sure he'll take a sick one. But he's going to take the best one he can find first. I've seen a lot of that.

Salmon Surveys

There are only a few places salmon can spawn and survive. I've flown fish surveys for years and I know they have to have fresh water burbling up. Like at Big Delta, chums go maybe a mile up the Delta River and that's as far as they go because it glaciers and freezes above that. They spawn right in the area where there's water burbling up all year and it never freezes solid. They have to have this water coming out of the ground to agitate the eggs and keep them fresh.

If the salmon went, say, into the Wood River, there's no place like that. No springs coming up, so they can't survive. It glaciers and freezes shut. If Fish and Game took eggs from someplace else, hatched them and put them into the Wood River, the fish would come back to there. It would be a whole separate run of salmon because that's the way they're programmed. The run wouldn't be self-sustaining because the spawn wouldn't live through the winter. New fish would have to be released every year. But you could have more fish and they wouldn't interfere with the natural spawning runs.

In this area quite a few kings go up the Salcha River, the Goodpasture, and the upper Tanana. Some go up the Chena and very few go up the Chatanika. There used to be a lot go

October, 1966. "I was in the guiding business, hauling moose hunters. I'm probably picking up a moose with the PA14. There's moose horns on the floats where we tied them on to bring them in."

The Chatanika River headed for Minto Flats. Al pointed out all the silt in the river from his plane. 1982.

p the Chatanika but when the mining started they ruined half the spawning round by running silt into the gravel or dredging it out. They just destroyed . Same in the Goldstream. There used to be salmon come up the Goldstream but the mining got rid of it all.

A lot of chums go up the Kantishna to the Toklat. They spawn at Knight's Roadhouse. The Nenana River has a lot of them go to around Clear. Then a ot of chums spawn right in the Tanana River between Harding Lake and Delta.

From the air, spawning areas are big gravel beds in the river where water prings are burbling up. You can see where the fish are hollowing out their ests with their tails. They brush a little hole out and lay their eggs in it. hen the males fertilize them and stay around to guard them. A lot of times more aggressive fish will chase off the first one and take over the nest. rom the air you can see all these fish laying in the spawning area guarding ests. They stay until they die. They use up all of whatever they got when hey leave the ocean, then die and float off.

Flying along there will be big schools of fish in certain areas milling round vying for position. When we do a count for a survey we start at the mouth of a stream and go up to the first school. The biologist generally has a ush button counter with him. He punches buttons for five, ten, or a hun- red fish, as many as there are. We fly around that first school until we ount every one of the fish. You're going to make mistakes, but basically you ount all of them.

Then you fly up to the next school and compare sizes. You get so you can udge pretty close. Going up the river I have to make every bend and fly as low as I can. I keep it at about two or three hundred feet altitude or whatever the weather will allow. As we follow the stream, the biologist is unching a button for whatever he figures is in the school. A little school ere, then a half mile up another little school. In a mile maybe a big school nd scattered ones in between.

On the Salcha we fly from the mouth all the way up. Most streams, though, glacier up at a certain point and there will be no more fish beyond that. In the Chandalar ninety per cent of the fish spawn just below Venetie. The Sheenjek is the same way. Thousands of them congregate right below one guy's trapping cabin there in a mile long stretch.

On a survey the biologist does the counting. The pilot has to concentrate on flying the airplane. It's a really tough job because you have to make all the bends going as slow as you can. For awhile the state bought a bunch of airplanes and their biologists flew them. But they had a problem crashing and killing so many people they went back to chartering. They figured the biologist was too interested in the project and didn't pay attention to the flying. Which was true. As a pilot I don't care if there are two fish or two thousand. But the biologist does. It's two different jobs.

That's why all these Cubs are augering in all the time. They're not watching what they're doing, make too tight a turn and auger it in. I really like the Heliocourier. There's no way you can auger that one in. The way the airplane is built it is stall proof and spin proof. It has special slats on the leading edge of the wing. When these slats come banging out, you know you have about another ten miles an hour to do something about it. In a conventional aircraft if you stall, you're going to spin. From that low altitude you have no chance to recover. But with the Helio it'll just straighten out. The nose will never go in. It'll always stay up so you'll fall flat if you do get into that predicament. But that's almost impossible. The chances of your getting hurt in a Helio are pretty remote. If you're in a Cub or 180, you're dead.

Chapter Three: Yukon Fish Camp

This chapter comes from an interview in 1983 at Al's fish camp three miles above the mouth of Hess Creek, twenty-five miles above Rampart on the Yukon River.

Commercial Fishing

Photo by Curt Madison

Ira Weisner, the trader in Rampart, used to sell canned fish all up and down the river. The best part of his cannery was his ice house. He dug it back into the hill about twelve feet wide and thirty feet long with bins on the side. In the winter he cut ice out of the Yukon to fill the bins. On the front he had double doors, insulated. When he was going in he'd open one door and close it, then open the other one. That way he didn't lose refrigeration.

As the first salmon started running, he'd buy them and stack them up in the ice house. They'd keep until he got two or three hundred, enough to start up his cannery. Then he'd hire women, mostly from Rampart, to cut the fish and put them in the cans. They sealed all the cans by hand and put them in his big commercial steam cooker. He could cook twenty cases at a time.

An airplane view of Hess Creek flowing into the Yukon River, 1982.

His business went pretty good selling up and down the river until the Health Department, or whichever government agency is trying to put you out of business, came over and put him out of business.

Nobody has ice houses like that anymore. I don't know why. They're the cheapest way to refrigerate anything in the world. Just leave them open in the winter at fifty below and they're cold all summer. Doesn't cost a penny to operate.

Storage is a real problem for commercial fishermen around here now. Everyone tried to get as many fish as they can during the openings. If the weather is bad a plane can't get in to pick them up so they throw them in the river on a line. Since the river temperature is maybe sixty degrees they're better off on the bank where it might be only fifty degrees. After a couple days when the plane can come in, the fish are already turning a little soft. Bum fish, where, you know, if people had ice houses they wouldn't have this problem.

At our camp we have a little stream running out of a creek down to the beach. The creek glaciers up in the winter and the ice doesn't all melt out until the middle of July. We just put a plastic pipe up into the ice water and run it into an old boat at the side of the river. The temperature of that water is about thirty-eight degrees. When we throw fish in there they could keep two or three days solid as can be. We check our nets twice a day and throw the fish in that water before cutting them. It's easier to cut strips out of firm fish.

I keep telling these fish buyers they ought to be selective about what they buy from the fishermen. If they turn down a few, then the fisherman will think twice before he mistreats a fish. Buyers know they can't sell junk fish. See, if somebody sells a large quantity of fish to a buyer he will take a few bad ones, but he won't turn them on the market. He'll use them himself or sell them to somebody who wants to can them. Buyers know that if they sell

Al Wright sitting on the beach of his fish camp on the Yukon River, 1982. Ice water from a nearby creek is piped into the boat to keep fish fresh until they can be cut.

38

junk fish to a consumer, they'll lose their market. That's what happened in Europe.

A few years ago the European market was established and the buyers wanted to get all the fish they could for it. They went up on the Yukon buying everything. If the weather was bad for a couple days and fishermen held the fish over, they'd buy them anyway because they needed the quantity. They hauled whatever they could get their hands on.

The next year buyers couldn't send fish to Europe. Think about it. When a guy gets a fish that cost him sixty or seventy dollars laying in front of him and it's rotten, he's pretty unhappy about it. You can't blame him. So Europe said no more, we don't want no more of that junk

Al and Jeanne Wright's fish camp three miles above Hess Creek on the Yukon River, 1982.

Al's son Jack pouring airplane gas at the family fish camp on the Yukon River, 1982.

Jack, Al and Jeanne on the porch of their fish camp cabin, 1982.

Yukon fish. And it wasn't junk to start with. Fishermen just made it that way after they caught it.

This camp here at Hess Creek we started about 1966, before that I used to fish on the Tanana. Mostly around Nenana or between there and Minto. I've always fished. Wheels and nets both.

Wheels are better for chums because chums are so hard to pull out of a net. A wheel will catch as many as you can use anyway so you're better off with a wheel if you're fishing chums. Right now we have net permits because we mainly fish for kings. With a net we can catch more kings and bigger ones.

My wife Jeanne and I come to the camp to fish for kings. My son Jack has a wheel permit he runs and our grandson Brook works with us up there, too. We don't fish chums much anymore ourselves. Jack does that. We just stay through the king season making strips and canning. We can kippered fish and fresh fish, whatever we think we'll need through the winter. We used to sell a few cans but the way things go nowadays we don't like to sell any because there are so many lawsuits. Since this last round with botulism in Bristol Bay we figure it just ain't worth it.

And it's a lot of work. You can make the same amount of money selling the fish fresh as you can if you smoke it and make salmon strips out of it. We get a dollar a pound for fresh fish in the round. If we took one of those fish and make it into strips, we have to cut them, strip them, salt them, hang them up for three weeks, take them down and only get ten dollars a pound. It comes out exactly the same because you only get one-tenth the weight out of the fish in strips as you get in the round. You're getting the same price as if you sold them in the round to start with and didn't do any of that work.

It used to be hard to sell fish on the upper Yukon. There were just a few guys come in with airplanes to buy. In the fifties and sixties Pete Merry and I used to come up and buy some for the local market in Fairbanks, but most everybody either made strips or put them up for themselves. It hasn't been

40

just till recent years that real commercial buyers have been moving in trying to buy fish. In the last five years now three or four buyers are operating on the upper Yukon.

We've been selling to Pierre Wakefield for the last four years. This year two other buyers moved in willing to pay a dollar ten a pound. He said he wouldn't have any hard feelings if we wanted to sell to someone else, but a dollar was all he could pay. I told him he'd been dealing with us for so long we would just keep selling to him even for ten cents a pound less. Try to help him out and keep him in business. We make enough off that so we don't have to worry about it. We just figure if prices get better we'll get more money, but if he goes out of business we ain't going to sell anything. If these other guys quit we know Pierre will be around. So we'd rather support him and keep him going.

We don't have the problem of giving our fish and then not getting paid for them, but I know some of these buyers run into that with the people they sell to in Seattle. Then some fishermen have problems with these fly-by-night buyers. They try to get more money out of their fish and they sell to somebody working on a shoestring. The guys we deal with we know real well. We know we're going to get paid no matter what. Even if they went broke, they'd work the rest of their life to pay us off because that's the kind of people they are. That's why we like to deal with them. If they say something, that's the way it is.

We know the buyers can't always keep their pick-up schedules so we say if the buyer doesn't show up by a certain time, we cut our fish into strips. 'Course we have an airplane, too, so I can fly the fish in myself to our freezer. We're not going to let them go down the tubes waiting. That's where you get bum fish. When the buyer shows up the next day, people throw all their fish together and you've got some lousy fish coming in. You have to get rid of the fish one way or another in a certain length of time. If nobody shows up to buy them, then you've got to cut them. A lot of people don't want to bother about cutting, because it's too much work.

Fishing Spots

Sometimes there are disputes about fishing spots. It's tough. Sometimes you have to resort to carrying a big stick. It used to be that a person had a fishing spot on the river and everybody would respect that. Nobody would bother them for years and years. Now all of a sudden with a big influx of people, everybody's trying to get in the good spots and they're having a lot of conflicts. We had a couple of people come up here but we told them we had been fishing this place for a long time and didn't appreciate them being in our eddy. Maybe they ought to move. They did.

Another thing, there is a couple, the Pitkas, living in Beaver. They come down to a camp a half mile above us every year. There's a first class fishing eddy right there. They show up about the Fourth of July to get subsistence fish for themselves. We made an agreement with them that we'd put a net in that eddy and use it while they were gone. That way we could hold it for them. The way the laws are now, you can't reserve a spot. Whoever's there first gets it. Pitkas have been there fishing for fifty years. Some years they come and some years they don't. If someone else put a net in there, Pitkas might come down and have no place to fish.

For the last ten years we have fished that eddy. When they come down they tell us and we pull our net out. When they leave we put it back in. That way there is no problem. It's a lot different than the old days. Just like traplines. Everybody respected where a guy trapped and didn't bother him. But nowadays nobody respects anybody's area. Some people do, but newcomers come in and think they can go anyplace. There's no law that says they can't. It comes down to whoever has the biggest stick gets the place.

Fishing Quotas

Before the road went through to the Yukon bridge there was no problem around us because it was so far to go. From Fairbanks you had to go two hundred seventy miles to Tanana, then a hundred miles up the Yukon to here. We were the only people here for years. When the road went through everybody started moving in. Now it's getting real crowded. Three new permits came in from off the Tanana this year just above us. One of the Biedermans from Eagle sold his permit to Sherry Madrow and a guy named Wieke brought in two from Nenana. It's going to be a bigger problem every year. There is such a limit to places where you can fish and so many people moving in.

The quota will stay the same so it means that each fisherman will get fewer fish. It'll be unprofitable to fish here anymore if you're trying to make it as a business. You won't be able to afford the equipment.

Most of the fish are caught in the ocean because those fishermen have got a lot of money behind them to hire lobbyists in Juneau to see that they get a big quota. They want all the fishing shut down on the rivers. They figure that if a fish gets into the Yukon, or any river, that fish should go spawn. But the people that live along the rivers don't think that way. They think those fish were put there to come back so they'd have something to eat through the winter. Everybody wants the fish. Whoever's got the most money and the most power gets the legislation to get the laws in their favor.

Ocean fishermen make so much more than a river fisherman that you can't even compare it. A man on the Yukon is lucky to make five thousand dollars in a year. A fisherman down at the mouth or in the ocean makes sixty to seventy thousand dollars in a year off the fish.

On the Yukon a lot of people depend on the fish for food. And just about everybody that fishes has dogs. I definitely think subsistence fishing should have preference over commercial. A subsistence fisherman is taking fish for his livelihood. A commercial fisherman is taking fish to make some profit and sell the fish to somebody who doesn't really need it.

Giving subsistence more priority means that the quota for ocean fishermen would be reduced, but it isn't necessary. If the resource was managed right there could be fish for everybody. Some of this money they're throwing away on useless things could be put into projects that benefit everybody like a hatchery or improved fish habitat. They could get twice as many fish coming up these rivers as there are right now. Then the fishermen in the oceans would get their quota and the people along the river would still have all the fish they needed.

It doesn't look very good for the future of commercial fishing on this stretch of the Yukon. There's getting to be so many people moving in and the quota is so small that you might be able to fish for only a week. You can probably still subsistence fish but if they get too many people subsistence fishing they're going to have to do something about that, too.

Right now you have to get a permit to subsistence fish this section of river. Anybody that wants to can go into Fairbanks to get one, but it means they already have a handle on it. Anytime they want they can start crimping down. They ask you how many fish you're going to catch and you have to tell them. Supposedly that's all you're supposed to catch then go get another permit if you want more. You have to keep a record of how many fish you caught. Then run that into them at the end of the season.

I think ten years from now the government will probably do away with the whole limited entry system. There is a big movement afoot by the fisheries on the coast to get rid of all the fishermen, commercial and subsistence, on the rivers. Then they could take more in the ocean and anything that escapes to the river will go spawn and make more salmon for them.

There's been a lot of talk about fishermen from around here getting together and forming some kind of association to try to make the fishing

Photo by Curt Madison

Al and his fish cutting table at the Wright's fish camp on the Yukon River, 1982.

Photo by Curt Madison

Dog salmon on drying racks at the Wright's fish camp.

better and more profitable, but nobody's got enough money to put into it. In order to do something you have to have a lobbyist go to Juneau and that costs a lot of money. If you just write them a letter, they ain't going to pay any attention to you. They'd just throw it in the wastebasket.

It is hard to do, too, because of the way they got this river chopped into different sections with different quotas. People fight for their own area and can't get together.

Regulations

Basically there's always a conflict between sports fishermen, commercial, and subsistence. They all think they should have all the fish. Politicians are trying to solve it but the way the government operates, they'll just make a big mess out of it and everybody will be mad. The main problem is they hire some kid just out of school who doesn't know what he's doing. And he's the guy that makes all the rules and regulations. He thinks he knows everything, but he doesn't have any idea what's going on. I know because I've worked with guys in the Fish and Game that have come out of some of their fancy schools. Just because I don't have a degree, I don't know anything.

They tell me all about what's going on with the animals and they think they've got it wired, but they don't know one lousy thing except what they read out of a book. And half the stuff they read in a book is wrong because the guy who wrote it didn't know nothing about it. But it's gospel once it's in writing. That's the way it is.

So they come out in the woods and some guy that's lived with these animals all his life tells them something and they say, "Oh, no. That's not right. It's this way." Well, you can't talk to them. And if you go to any of their meetings and bring your ideas they won't listen to you because you don't have a degree. They just flat won't listen to you. I've preached and preached to a lot of them about different animals and stuff.

One guy I started out from scratch with and flew him all over the country studying animals. He got mad at me and wouldn't fly with me anymore because I was always trying to tell him he was wrong. After about ten years he told me I was right about the things I was telling him. It took him ten years to figure it out. So that's the kind of people that are doing all your managing of fish and game. Then by the time they do learn anything they kick them out and get somebody else. The circus starts all over again.

It's pretty discouraging for people in a village. I used to fly these government people to villages. Hundreds of them to all the villages. They'd show up and walk around town and all they'd be is government paid tourists. That's what it amounted to. They'd come to a village, talk to people, and say they were going to do this and that. Of course, the villagers know better because they've seen so many of them come and go. They promise them this and promise them that. Then they go away and people never hear from them again. It's the same over and over and over. So pretty quick anybody that comes, they don't pay any attention. People know they're all lying. They're just in there for an airplane ride and to look at their village so what's the use of listening to any of them. They're just making a big noise. I've seen it happen for a long time.

Years ago there was no welfare. Now things are different. It's simple to see what happens. When you have to do something to live you do it. No matter what you have to do to live you're going to work hard. You're going to go out and get something to eat. But if somebody wants to give you something, why should you go out and work for it? It's just human nature. Anybody does that.

When I was first flying up here welfare was just starting to come around. I'd fly trappers out to their lines and about all they could make was their airplane fare and enough to buy their groceries while they were trapping. The government started giving welfare out, but a lot of them didn't want to take it. If they trapped and got just a little welfare they could make it. But if you went trapping, you were employed and couldn't qualify for welfare whether you made any money or not.

I went to BIA and said why don't you let these people that want to trap, go. Then if they don't make enough, give them a little bit. Say they need a hundred dollars a month to live on and they only get sixty dollars worth of fur. Then give them forty dollars. Instead they say don't go trapping at all and collect one hundred dollars. Pretty quick everybody finds out it's way easier to go collect welfare than it is to go trapping or hunt. Why not go home and sit in the village and collect the welfare and you don't have to do all that work. That's basically what it's all about. How everything went to hell. See, the government won't subsidize an operation, but they want to give everything away. It changes everybody's life. Once people get dependent on it what are they going to do?

One guy told me he's so at ease, "I don't have to depend on nobody for a living. The only thing I got is my welfare check." He figures that's coming to him and there's no end to it. He doesn't have to do nothing or depend on anybody cause he's getting a welfare check.

Now there's a lot of people that don't do that. They still get out and work and they've never really been on welfare. They do jobs around the village. One thing and another. They're workers. People that don't care to work, don't have to work. It's always been that way in the villages. There'd be a few producers. Two or three guys would get the bulk of the game and give it to the rest of the people. Now it's getting to be more and more where nobody wants to share nothing. They just get it for themselves unless it's a potlatch or something. That's the way society is changing.

It's impossible to ever go back to the old way of life any more. No way it could happen. Mainly because there's too many people and too few resources to take care of them. If all the Natives in Alaska tried to go back to a sub-sistence way of life, they'd all starve to death. In the old days there were very few people compared to what there are now. And they spread out over a big area.

Minto people came over as far as Fairbanks and there weren't very many of them. Just about five or six families. And a family would pick up and move to wherever they had to go to catch what they needed. Like old Justin Frank, Richard Frank's father, had a trapline from Minto right across the Sawtooth Mountains down Hess Creek into the Yukon and back around. He fished over on the Yukon during the summer with a wheel for his dogs and stuff. People covered a big territory. They never stayed in one place. They couldn't. It was impossible to live in one place and survive.

People did that all over. They scattered over the Yukon Flats and up into Canada. In the summer they had gathering places like White Eye at the mouth of Birch Creek. They'd have a big fish trap and catch salmon. Take it easy all summer. Then come fall they'd pack up their gear, each family, and head out. Take what they could with them and try to make a living through the winter.

That's how those caches in the Minto Flats got built. It was a place everybody gathered in the spring to catch fish. They'd put in a weir across the creek and the whole village would come there. They'd catch fish in a cooperative effort and put them away. If you'll look at any village in the country you'll find that they stopped where they can get fish. Because they could always depend on getting fish. Other game would be scarce a lot of times but they knew they could get fish.

But now it's impossible to go back to the subsistence way. Some people say they want to but they can't. In the first place they wouldn't know how to do it. They wouldn't know how to gather it. All those ways that they did things are lost except to a few of the old people. But they'd never do it again. It's too much work. It's too hard. Everybody says it was an easy life, but it ain't. They worked from daylight till dark every day to make a living.

It's a lot of work to take care of your own food. Because you're not mass producing it like the food in the stores. To make three pounds of jerky you you have to start with fifteen pounds of meat. You have to make a brine to salt it a little bit then build a smokehouse and hang it in there for about four days to dry it out. It takes time. But the hard thing is cutting it into all the thin strips so it'll dry good.

We catch moose and caribou and use everything. Jeanne cans a lot of it so we don't buy any commerical meat. Once in awhile we buy pork chops or chicken, but ninety-five percent of our meat we get ourselves. Moose, caribou, fish, sheep, ducks, geese. Then Jeanne picks a lot of berries and raises a garden and greenhouse. Actually we're about as self-sufficient food-wise as we can get nowadays and still operate.

It used to be that you were able to just go and get what you wanted anytime you wanted it. Nowadays if you want to go get something you're afraid all the time that somebody's going to catch you in the wrong place or doing the wrong thing and you're going to get in trouble over it. You're living in fear all the time where before you didn't have to do that. You were free. You could go out and have fun while you were hunting. Now you don't know if you're in a closed area or an open area half the time. Or whether the season's open or not. You have to study the regulation for a week before you're sure you're in the right place. Then you're still not sure. That's the main thing I don't like. You don't know what you're doing wrong.

For instance, this summer after they closed the commercial king season we

Photo by Curt Madison

Al and Jeanne's camp at Minto Flats, 1982. Caches can be seen at center left.

pulled our nets for twenty-four hours. Then we can fish subsistence. We did that. A Fish and Game enforcer came along and landed by our nets. I ran down and caught him in the boat. I asked him what he was doing. He told me it was a closed period. I said it wasn't and he kept saying it was. So I brought him up to the camp to show him in his own book. We were right and he was wrong. If the Fish and Game don't even know their own regulations, how do they expect us to know them?

Caches in the Minto Flats.

One of the rules is that nets have to be out by six o'clock before a closed period. All right, naturally you try and leave them in as long as you can. You figure it will take an hour to pull the nets and you start out at five o'clock. Then you run into a problem at one of the nets with big drift so you don't have it out until seven or eight o'clock. You're worried to death in the meantime that while the net's still in the river they're going to come by and confiscate it. You shouldn't have to live under those kinds of pressures. Everybody along the river is in the same boat.

Finally people get to the point where they say, "Fish and Game changes the rules so much why should we live by any of their rules or regulations? They don't know what they're doing themselves." But if you don't follow their rules they take all your stuff away from you. If they catch you. They're trying to make criminals out of everybody.

Before you could go out and fish and catch what you wanted. You didn't worry about nothing. You were just sitting here fat, dumb, and happy. Now you're all up-tight and getting ulcers over catching a couple fish or shooting a moose.

Al skinning a moose on a lake in the Minto Flats 1966.

We started out years ago in Nenana with a canoe and rowboat for checking the wheel. The equipment progressively got better. Boats are better and don't break down anymore. Now we've got a Lowline eighteen-foot boat with a thirty-five horse Evinrude outboard. It's easy to run and take care of. We have a little boom lift with an electric motor to pull our net anchors so we don't pull them by hand anymore. We have a depth finder so we can check the depth of the water so we know where to set the nets without sounding for them. It makes things a lot easier. And we need to get easier because I can't handle that heavy work anymore. It's getting to me. But something would definitely be missing from my life if I couldn't get my own food. I know if things really got tough and you couldn't get food from someplace else I'd still know how to get my own and take care of it. I wouldn't live good maybe, but I could get by.

An old cache at Caches, Minto Flats 1982.

Chapter Four: Fly-In Fish Camp

Sport Fishing

We have a place in the Minto Flats we take sportsmen for pike fishing. I built the first cabin there in 1966, but we had tents set up before that. Finally we just gave up on tents because the bears tore them up all the time. The season starts there in June so before that Jeanne and I spend a couple weeks getting it all fixed up. Then we get our operation ready for king salmon fishing on the Yukon about the first of July. Jeanne stays on the Yukon with my son Jack. I fly back and forth hauling fish from the Yukon and people into the Minto camp. Back and forth. I'm just flying all around plus I take any other charters if all the other pilots are busy. I fill in and keep everything organized.

We have a package deal to the cabins on the Flats. We furnish people the transportation in and out and a cabin with a boat and a motor. They bring their own groceries and fishing gear. The cabins are set up for cooking and everything to just move in. We sell them the package. We take them in one morning, they stay overnight, and

Photo by Curt Madison

Wright's pike fishing camp on the Little Goldstream in the Minto Flats 1982.

we bring them back the next night. That gives them two days of fishing. Sometimes people want to stay longer so they just pay for the extra days. I try to arrange to bring one group in when I bring another out, but usually that doesn't work out and I have to make a trip in and out for the same people. Then in the falltime we haul in duck hunters. The camp can hold twelve people but we average eight. There are probably about a hundred fifty total during the season.

It works out good for the air service because it is a short trip and we can work it in amongst other trips. Counting ground time it only takes about an hour round trip. Then I have to go in there and fix the motors. Even if I put new motors in there, people will screw them up. I have to go about one day a week and fix everything.

Most of the people we take in are local Fairbanks people. People that have been there before and want to go back. We get quite a few tourists but we don't do any advertising. It's all word of mouth. We don't try to make a big deal out of it. The place won't stand very much pressure. It's actually getting too much fishing pressure right now from all the pilots around Fairbanks. Plus there are two or three other guides taking fishing parties in there. It's getting overfished, really, right now. We just take in a few. Don't try to push it. Just keep a few people there to keep the camp intact.

I built three cabins but the camp's been there for as long as I know. Minto people gathered up there in the spring from all around the Flats. The camp's right in that point where the big Minto Lake and Goldstream come together, just above the Chatanika. Everybody coming out of the Flats in the spring with their canoes would land there.

That's why there are a bunch of old caches right across from my camp. Most of them are tumbling down now but in the early

Al Wright filleting a pike in front of one of his Minto Flats rental cabins, 1982.

One of Al and Jeanne's pike fishing cabins in the Minto Flats.

days each family had one of these caches to store their stuff. When they'd leave the Flats to go to the river, anything they didn't need they left in the cache. When they came back the next year it would be there. Nobody ever bothered anything.

Everything is stripped out now. There was nothing of real value, just the stuff that people used to use long ago. After about 1950 nothing was left there. See, after people got motor boats, and airplanes came around, they didn't use the caches much.

Right after freeze-up people used that place, too. They would cut a hole in the ice at Caches and catch pike like they were going out of style. Stack them up like cordwood, freeze them and haul them into the village to feed dog teams. I flew people in there and tons of fish out.

Al's float plane at Caches in the Minto Flats.

There're still four or five families that come up to Caches in the spring and set nets around for pike and whitefish. Hunt muskrats and stuff. Peter John comes up and Matthew and Dorothy Titus. Susie Jimmy comes up and Ike Edwin. Jim Alexander and Evelyn always come.

Quite a few people out of Fairbanks have duck hunting cabins on the big lake. It is all state land now. Minto village corporation tried to get it under ANCSA but they couldn't. They were allowed just so much land and they had to claim the township around the village. A lot of them have Native Land Claims homesteads in there. That's how I got mine. There are probably a dozen cabins around the lake owned by businessmen in Fairbanks. They use them for duck hunting in the fall.

For awhile there was a problem with a bunch of radical kids coming out on the Flats and breaking up camps. They wiped me out a couple of times. It's getting better now. They would go to the duck camps around the big lake and burn them down. Cops would come and catch them. They'd go to court in Fairbanks, get turned loose and go do the same thing again.

I don't blame people for being angry. Minto Lake had always been a prime hunting area for Minto. But I think there were only four or five kids actually wrecking the duck camps. They wanted to chase the White people out of the Flats and go back to the subsistence life. That's impossible. They just don't understand how hard life was in the old days. And legally, they couldn't claim the land under the Alaska Native Claims Settlement Act. Everyone in the state has equal access to it.

Minto got a reputation for being a rough place when most of the people are friendly. The worst damage to our camp was caused by people coming out of the Chatanika River. One year they stole everything in camp — the canoe, dishes, everything. We found some of our dishes in a cabin on the Chatanika a couple years later.

Just above where I'm at is an old camping ground and an Indian graveyard. They call it Graveyard Camp. That's the place I was telling you I went with my dad by dog team to funerals and weddings. Another lake they call Four Cabins where my grandmother used to live. No cabins there now but there used to be. Right down from here a little ways is a big deep hole really good for pike fishing in the fall. There were little spots like that around where these people used to get out most of their fish certain times of the year.

Subsistence Priority

Carlos Frank shot a moose for a potlatch out of season. I think it was stupid of Fish and Game to arrest him for that. People have been getting moose for potlatch ever since time started. 'Course when they make a law, I guess you're supposed to live by it. But if there's a potlatch I don't care how many laws the government makes they ain't going to stop people from going and getting a

Photo by Curt Madison

Pike fish fillets just cut by Al Wright at one of his Minto Flats cabins, 1982.

moose. All these laws are made for a purpose, I'll grant you, but when you try to change somebody's way of life with a law that ain't going to stop them from doing something.

You know Natives are using all that meat they hunt. They aren't just killing it for the hell of it. Like all these people that go along the highway and shoot a moose and leave it lay. I can see they really ought to get tough with them. But for somebody that's utilizing it, like those Natives, they shouldn't do anything. It's hard to do, though. It's hard to overlook the law for one person and not for another. If Natives are living like Whitemen I guess they got to live by their rules. But it's hard to do. I live by my rules too, not only what the government tells me to do.

It's the same in the Interior around Minto or any of these villages. People killed what they could get. I know when I was a kid we used to go with my dad and he'd kill twenty to thirty caribou at one time in the fall. We'd dress them out and pile them up. Then we come back and haul them with the dog team. We used them to eat and for dog food and everything. He did that because the caribou would only come through once in the fall and once in the spring. We didn't have to kill as many in the spring because we had other things. Ducks were coming back and fish. But in the fall you got what you needed for all winter. Trappers did the same thing.

There were lots of caribou then. Hunters didn't deplete the herds. Sickness and predators killed off the caribou. The way Native people managed game, they only took what they needed. On a trapline they only took as much fur as they felt they needed then quit trapping. They wouldn't clean out a beaver house. They just take two big ones and leave the rest. Most of these White trappers tried to get everything. Clean it out because they were after the money. 'Course some of them did it just like the Natives did. They left animals in their country.

In the old days all these Natives people were interested in was making a living. They just took what they needed. They knew that if they left fur animals, they were going to be there next year. It was healthy for the animal population that way because they took the older, bigger animals and the new ones could keep coming.

These new game laws just make outlaws out of us. We're going to hunt anyway. We can't change the way we live. After we've been doing this for over fifty years we aren't going to change overnight. We'll have to do the best we can and hope they don't catch us. Or fight back if they do catch us. This subsistence business is all rules that the government made to protect the Native's right to hunt and fish. Well, when they do that they violate the state constitution. It's wrong no matter which way they do it. If they take away the subsistence laws then all the people that live out in the bush won't be able to live very good. They can't go out and catch fish or meat whenever they need it. And they can't afford to live any other way.

In towns and cities people are not so dependent on game because they have other ways of making a living. They buy most of their stuff and hunt for sport. Then there are a lot of people just like me who don't need the meat. We could go buy it but we don't like to buy that stuff. We like to take care of our own meat. Take care of it in the way we always have. You'd have to live altogether different otherwise. Maybe this younger generation will change, but we won't.

Legally, right now, subsistence priority means that if there is a lack of game animals, sport and commercial uses get cut back first. Some regulations prohibit transportation of hunters or meat by private airplane or close off areas to motorized vehicles. And seasons are set to favor local residents. The Minto Flats moose season begins the day after Labor Day weekend so people in Fairbanks can't use their extra time off to go there.

These laws are a result of the Alaska National Interest Lands Act that established all the big National Parks. They wanted to help keep subsistence living as a viable way of life. A lot of sportsmen's groups are against it. They say the law violates the state constitution which gives all citizens equal access to game. People will argue about that for a long time. For rural people there is no choice. They must have game animals to survive.

The way I see it, if the subsistence priority was repealed and everyone given equal access when game was low, the guy living in Anchorage or Fairbanks would be able to hunt say one week out of the year and a guy living here on the Yukon would only be able to hunt one week out of the year for his meat. For the guy in Anchorage he can go out and get a moose and take it back and put it in his freezer and live on it. But the guy out in the woods can't do that. He doesn't have any refrigeration to keep it. The only way he can keep it is to dry it. So he uses a lot more of it. If he needs a moose or a fish he's going to go get it when he needs it. That's the only way he can live out in the bush. If they repeal the subsistence law and make everybody live by the rules and regulations for sports hunting and fishing the people in the

Photo by Curt Madison

Al with his son Jack checking over a bear skin at their Yukon River Fish camp.

Al and Jeanne Wright Collection

"Glenn Grismann with a sixty-five and a half inch moose he got when I was guiding. September 1969 at one of the hunting camps I had in the Alaska Range."

bush will just have a tough time.

The reason there's not enough game is strictly the government's fault. They could build these herds up but they don't want to do it. They want to keep them under control. Every time a herd starts building up they kill it off. They annihilate it. Get it down to where there's nothing again so they can say you have to have permits, high license fees, and tags. Bunch of bureaucratic crap. If they managed it right there'd be plenty.

They send some kid to school. He reads out of a book all the mistakes that somebody else made and thinks they're all the true laws. So he tries to administer the laws like that and people that live in the bush won't even listen to them.

Before the White people showed up, the Indians had better conservation laws than they have now. When I was hauling all the trappers around the Minto Flats in the spring, they knew how the muskrat population was doing. The government had seasons but a lot of times people would close off their season a week ahead. They'd have a meeting amongst themselves and say we're taking too many muskrats. We got to quit hunting and leave the rest. They'd all agree and stop killing with a week to go yet on the government season. Late in the spring, too, the rat skins weren't much good because they're getting all chewed up. They don't want to take them. Leave them go for next year.

There used to be a big rat population in Minto Flats. I hauled five or six thousand skins a year out of there. Now they get maybe three or four hundred. Mining contributed a lot to the downfall of the rats. They poured mud into the Chatanika and Goldstream and it just filled up the lakes killing off the feed. They're still pumping that mud in there. Even with all the environmental crap going today they're still pumping mud into the Flats and killing off the lakes.

Photo by Curt Madison

Al with salmon gill nets.

59

Miners will say the silt's not hurting anything but I can show you good lakes that now are willow patches with muddy little streams going through them. Pumping mud into the Yukon or Tanana or some stream that doesn't have fish in it doesn't hurt anything, but you have to be careful in places like the Flats.

Water in the big Minto Lake is getting shallower every year. See, all the mud backs up in there during the high water and then it settles out and the clear water drains off depositing the mud. Natives in Minto have been hollering and crying about that ever since I can remember. Ever since I was a little kid when the FE was mining, they sent delegates to Fairbanks to try to get something done about filling in those lakes with mud. Nobody'd listen to them. They just threw them out. The people could see their land going to hell, but nobody cared.

Now everybody says they care about this and care about that, but the mud is still being pumped in. What are you going to do? Scream and holler but it doesn't do any good. The only thing you can do is go back to the old Wild West days I guess, if you want to get something done.

All that silt has a tremendous effect on the ducks and muskrats. Beaver are doing good because they move around quite a bit and they eat willows so it doesn't bother them. Actually it's good for them as long as they got enough water to build a house. But for the muskrats and waterfowl it is a different story. Silt destroys all their feed. Lakes fill in so the muskrat grass won't grow anymore. A different kind of grass takes over. Then the lakes shallow up and freeze to the bottom so the muskrats freeze out. Some lakes that used to have fish in them are barren now because the fish die from lack of oxygen. Naturally this affects the people in Minto a lot. It means there is less food.

"That's me skinning a muskrat up on the Yukon Flats, 1968. Muskrats were all over that lake. we had a ball."

Minto Flats.

Chapter Five: Hawaii

This chapter is taken from an interview March 1980 at Al and Jeanne's house in Kona, Hawaii.

A Warm Place

There was an old guy named Boatman who lived at Totchaket, the place I was telling you we went fishing. He raised potatoes. One year while we were living in Minto towards the end of winter we ran short of groceries so Dad was taking a couple days to go up to Boatman's place to get some potatoes.

I decided the day he was coming back to go out the trail and meet him. I walked and walked. I must have walked five miles and I was starting to get tired wondering what happened to him, you know, that he never showed up. So I got to dreaming.

I dreamed that I was going across this lake and kind of day-dreaming I fell down a hole. Down under the lake was a beautiful land. Beautiful green summer, nice and warm. It wasn't cold any more. And it was this place, Hawaii, I was dreaming about. I didn't know it until we got here forty years later. I had no idea any place like this existed. Jeanne ran a travel service along with the air service up in Fairbanks. We'd get free trips once or twice a

Al Wright and his producing banana trees at his home in Kona, Hawaii. March 1985.

year. We started traveling all over the world to see what was going on. We decided we should be finding a warm place to get out of the cold winters as we got older. We looked all over for someplace to go.

In most places there's a foreign government and you don't know what's going to happen. Here it's an American owned place and the same customs we're used to. So we decided on Hawaii. Plus it has the best climate of any place.

Then we started going from one island to another to find the best one to live on. We liked it in Kona on the Big Island because it was a small community and there was good hunting and fishing. It fit in with our way of life. We looked around for a lot and built this house in 1973.

Before we decided on Hawaii we went all over. We went to Mexico, South America, the Carribean, the Canary Islands. We were in Fiji, Africa, India, and Japan. We even went to Russia. We got to some of the Scandanavian countries and Italy. We've been around to a few places, but no place was as good as here. Except maybe Rhodesia. It was pretty nice. It had a lot of things we liked, animals and a good climate. But the political situation has all gone to pot.

We always had in mind looking for a place that was warm. We had some friends who bought some land in Mexico. They were going to build themselves up a place there. But after two or three years the government came and took it away from them. They got their money back but they didn't make anything on it. That's an example of what we didn't want. The climate in these other places was either too hot or too cold or too rainy. We felt Hawaii was the right place.

Kona has grown up a lot. There were only four houses nearby when we got here and no stoplights downtown. You could stop along the road and talk to somebody and nobody got excited if you blocked the road for ten minutes. Everybody knew everybody. It's unbelieveable how fast it grew. About as fast as Fairbanks, you know. When we first came it was just like living in the woods.

63

Alaska has changed the same way. Fairbanks has moved from being a small place to being a city. I go downtown and if I see somebody I know, it's a miracle. It used to be that I knew everybody on the street.

There are just too many people in the world. They've got to have a place to go and they're all looking for the same thing. They find a good place and go there. Everybody's got the same idea so you end up right back where you started. It's a never ending cycle.

There are all kinds of people in Kona from Alaska. Every year they have a picnic and about two hundred people show up just living in this area. Some of them are retired and stay here year round, but most of them come down for three or four months in the winter just the same as we do. I don't think we'll ever live here permanently because we like Alaska too much in the summer. But since there's not much doing there in the winter for us we figure it's better to be here.

We go out hunting up on the mountain a couple times a year for sheep or pigs. We always get a turkey or two for Christmas dinner. There are other game birds that are good, too. If you want to hunt easy for pigs you take dogs to corner them. Otherwise you have to stay in the open country or you'll never see the pig. You can hear them run in the thick brush but you can't see them. It's a little different hunting here than in Alaska because you can't use hunting dogs there. And you have to go a long ways to get different things. In Hawaii everything is close.

Fishing in Kona is all salt water and mostly trolling. You can throw some lures over the back of the boat and troll for marlin or mahi-mahi or ahi or ono. Then you can bottom fish on long hand-lines, too. But the bottom is so deep it takes a long time to get the line down a couple thousand feet. And it's a lot of work unless you have an electric reel which we don't. So far we've caught ahi, aku, kawa-kawa, mahi-mahi, ono, opakapaka, gray snapper, and lots of little shore fish. There are a lot of fish here I don't know the name of.

One Christmas Jeanne got me a throw net and a friend of mine taught me how to use it. There's quite an art to it. You have to sneak up on the fish. You can't just walk out there and throw it. You find out where the fish are and then wait for the right kind of wave to come along to boil the water so the fish can't see the net. Then you throw it and hope you catch something. The net has weights all around the sides and pockets. Fish swim in the pockets trying to get out. You generally catch a few.

I've done a little spear fishing, too, just using a snorkle, not with scuba gear. I go in shallow water but I have an ear problem and can't stay in very long before it starts hurting.

Boats here are different than in Interior Alaska. A flat bottom boat here would beat itself to death on the waves. They're all v-bottomed to take the waves better. And once you leave the shore it's a thousand feet deep so you don't have to worry about running your propeller up on a bar.

We've hooked onto a couple sharks but we never brought one in. They always cut the line on us. You have to have an ahi line with a wire leader to catch a shark because their teeth are so sharp. They can cut through an ordinary line without worrying about it. We lose lures to sharks once in awhile.

White-tipped sharks are supposed to be good to eat and some people get them. Every once in awhile they have a shark come in along the beaches and they warn people to not go in the water while they're around. Everybody's scared of them.

I have a friend who used to do a lot of diving. He said they had one shark, a great white, that they'd go down and feed. They caught fish for him and fed him for about a month. He was getting tame. But pretty quick he wanted more than they

Papayas at Al and Jeanne's Kona home.

65

could catch. They started getting scared of him. The shark would come to them every time they'd dive. If they didn't catch any fish, they were afraid he was going to eat them instead. Finally they fed him a can of lye and did him in. He was getting too aggressive. But my friend told me all you have to do is keep facing the shark all the time. If they come too close just bang them on the nose. They won't bother you. But if they come from behind you, they'll get you. I don't know if it's true or not. That's what he claimed. I'd just as soon not face one.

We've planted a lot of things around this place. Papayas, macadamia nuts, avocados, and bananas. All things that we can use. We planted a bunch of citrus fruits and the grapefruit is bearing now. The oranges, tangerines, lemons, and limes should start later. We planted the avocado about four years ago and the graft is just starting to take now.

With all the different things we grow, there is always something coming on. It gives us something to do and it's interesting. A lot of people that have a place in Hawaii won't grow even one kind of producing tree or fruit. It seems like a waste of good ground to me because all you have to do it put it in. We've got lots of flowers and bushes and stuff around here for ornamental stuff. But everything I plant is something to eat. Jeanne puts the trimmings around.

My friend, Jimmy Matsumoto, showed me how to do grafting. Just like everything else there are tricks to it. You have fifty failures for every success. I try different ways to see how it is going to work. One guy up the hill has a citrus tree with an orange, grapefruit, lemon, and lime all on the same tree.

The coconut tree isn't doing too good because we just cleared this lot by hand. Over there on our other lot we used a Cat to break up the rocks a little. The papaya tree is doing really well there. The bananas have four stalks coming on next to the smokehouse.

I smoke marlin in the smokehouse. Most people use a hot smoke but I like

Stalk of bananas almost ready for harvest.

the cold smoke just like on our salmon. The fire is down low and the racks are high so we get lots of smoke but not much heat. Over here we use kiawe or guava wood.

There are a lot of problems trying to live in two different places with two houses. For one we can't have pets because we can't bring them into Hawaii. A dog or a cat would have to be in quarantine for sixty days so it wouldn't do any good to bring them. We had a couple of pets, a cat and a dog. We still have the cat. He doesn't care about our leaving because cats could care less about people anyway. But the dog was hard to leave. Every once in awhile a stray will come along here and Jeanne will say, "Let's keep him. That's a nice dog." But we can't do it. Our grandson brought a dog home the other day and wanted to keep him so bad, but we couldn't do it. We had to haul him back up on the hill and dump him off where we found him.

Then, of course, you have to find somebody to live in your house. If they don't take care of it, it costs you more than if you'd just locked it up. But you don't dare do that because somebody'd come in and clean you out. Take everything you got. And in Alaska you have to keep the heat on. It's not good for a house to leave it empty in the winter because it frosts up. Then if you have a water softener you have to drain it or take it out. And you have to drain all your plumbing. We designed our house to do that, but when it came time we found we couldn't close it down. It was too big of a problem.

When we leave here we're going back to Seattle to tend to some business. Then we're going to visit Jeanne's folks for about a week in New York. We'll be back to Fairbanks about the fifteenth of April to go back to work so we can do it again.

Going back to Alaska when it's cold and miserable takes a little getting used to. But coming the other way is no problem at all. The first couple days on the beach you have to be careful. But after we get a bit of a tan it doesn't bother so much.

When we were living in Alaska, we just expected to put up with all the cold of winter. We prepared for it and didn't worry about it. But now when we see that forty and fifty below coming we think it looks pretty good over in Kona. We think we better go.

Actually the way we live it's cheaper for us to live here through the winter than in Fairbanks. We have no fuel bills and our biggest expense is gasoline because we raise most everything we need. Then we bring moosemeat and salmon with us to last the year. We dig a lot of clams in Alaska and bring them down. With what we hunt on the mountain and the fish we catch here we never buy meat. And around here people always divide out fresh stuff from their gardens. If we take down a bunch of bananas, we split it with our neighbors and they give us fresh fruits and vegetables when they have them. We trade kippered salmon for avocados. It works out pretty good.

Actually the people that have been here a long time, that live here, are just like Alaskan people. They're all friendly and want to get along. Seems like the only problems come from people that move here and bring their own customs with them. Basically the customs here are the same as in Alaska.

Our friend, Jimmy Matsumoto is Japanese and his wife is Chinese. When they have dinner for Chinese New Year they invite everybody. It's just like going to a potlatch in Minto. There are all kinds of Native-type foods and stuff. It's just a big get-together and everybody has a good time.

Actually with the changes around here lately, it's mostly just small groups that still do that kind of exchanging. When you get to downtown Kona it is just like a city again. People don't say hello to you or nothing when you meet them on the street. They just look at you like, "What are you doing here?" Where it used to be that even if you didn't know people they were still friendly. It's getting to the point that they aren't friendly anymore.

Too many people coming in. It's like a big city now. You live your whole life and don't know who your neighbor is. Even in this subdivision. We used to know everybody here, but now we don't know hardly anybody. We have our own friends we visit back and forth, but we don't meet new people like we used to.

When a guy first moved here and needed some help pouring a driveway or something, everybody came over to help. Now I don't see much of that anymore. Too many people. It's the same way in Alaska. Even in smaller towns like Nenana. I grew up there but now when I go to Nenana I only know one or two people out of everybody I see. They're all different people in there. The only place you see the same ones is in isolated villages and even Minto has people I don't know. Villages haven't changed much because there is nothing for anybody else to do if they did move there.

Kona is changing mostly because of the climate. They're building two more big hotels downtown. I think they'll have six hundred rooms between them. That'll bring a lot more people. I don't know. If it gets where there's a traffic light on every stop, maybe we'll be moving back to Alaska permanently.

Kona, all of Hawaii, is really dependent on tourists. We had a little recession and tourism was down twenty percent for the last two months. It hurts the businesses. But the thing that's made this grow so much is mainly people, retired people moving in here. They build houses and the property value goes out of sight. A place you could buy for fifteen thousand dollars three years ago is fifty thousand now. Just for a little bitty one-quarter acre with nothing on it.

Young people have a really tough time here. They've got no way to get a house, unless they have folks with lots of money who want to buy them one. If they're starting out working, it's impossible for them to buy a house on wages. Just flat impossible.

The only future for us here is a good place to spend the winter to get out of the cold and snow. We'll probably keep doing it as long as we can get back and forth.

I thought about having a business down here. In fact, in 1976 I bought Kona Flight Service and started running it. But every time we'd let someone else take care of it, it'd go downhill again. We finally decided it wasn't feasible. I had enough worry about taking care of the one up in Alaska. We had a good tour going around the island, charter service and flight school. But it was too much work to build it up again each time we came back. We finally sold it last year.

The only reason we can come down here for as long as we do is that I have a partner running the show in Fairbanks. Bob Bursiel is a young fellow. He has flown with me for about ten years. At the time I started this Wright Air Service I had three kids flying for me. I incorporated and gave them each a share in it. We were all equal. Then the corporation was buying me out. The other two fizzled out but Bob stuck with it. He owns half the air service now. He runs it, but I go up and help him out in the summer. That way I don't have to be so tied down to it twelve months of the year. Generally he takes a two week vacation while I'm in Alaska, but he's right back. He's young and eager.

Al and Jeanne flying over the Minto Flats, 1982.

Epilogue

February 22, 1985. We checked over this manuscript with Al and Jeanne. They added this update.

The air service is still called Wright's but we sold our share out to Bob two years ago. We own the planes and lease them to him. We continue to fish with Jack and Brooke on the Yukon. And we still run the camp at Caches in Minto Flats. About five miles away from the camp we built our own cabin. That one we don't rent out. Peter John named the slough we built on "Rotten Slough" because swamp gas bubbles up through it.

We've added another bedroom onto the house in Kona to make that place more comfortable. Our macademia nut trees and avocadoes are producing so well now we plan to take the produce to the Farmer's Market. People sell things out of the backs of their trucks at a place across from Keahou Gardens. We figure we can make expense money doing that.

I got an old PA-12 airplane in Fairbanks. Tommy Kushida and I are completely rebuilding it. We're putting in a 180 engine, wing flaps, and taking out the rear controls. It will have a big comfortable pilot's seat. Everything I've wanted in a bush plane for hunting.

The future looks like steady motoring back and forth between Fairbanks and Kona and trying to grow, catch and hunt as much of our own food as possible. That's important to us no matter where we're living.

Al's set up for shelling his macadamia nuts at his Kona home 1985.

Al and Jeanne Wright at one of their Minto Flats fishing cabins, 1982.

Al and Jeanne's home on the Chena River in Fairbanks, 1983.

71

Al handling a winch at his Yukon River fish camp.

Al sitting by the creek at his Yukon River fish camp.

Al's set up for heating water for showers at their Yukon River fish camp.

Photo by Yvonne Yarber

L-r: Eric Charlie, "Lefty" Leonard Jimmie, Al Wright, Jeanne Wright, Edmond Titus and Pat Isaacson at a political campaign party for Jules Wright in Manley Hot Springs 1984.

Photo by Yvonne Yarber

L-r: "Link" Wright, Jeanne Wright, Al Wright and Cy Hetherington at Jules Wright's 1984 campaign party at his home in Manley Hot Springs.

73

1985 aerial of Minto village looking north with the water plant in the foreground.

Geneway Frank, Tony John and Peter John taking care of moosemeat in Minto Flats 1985.

74

Peter John's grandson Tony's first moose. Tony and Geneway cut it up while Peter John gives instructions.

photo by Yvonne Yarber

Elsie John and Ellen Frank at fall camp in 1985 at Minto Flats removing porcupine quills for later use in fur sewing. The porcupine meat was later eaten.

Al Wright at the microphone presiding over the Tanana Chiefs first regional Elders Conference held at Minto 1982. L-r: Lillian Olin, Poldine Carlo, Neal Charlie, Al Wright, Jim Demientieff.

Index

Al Wright

The *Yukon-Koyukuk Biography* Series

Available from Spirit Mountain Press

Edgar Kallands - Kaltag	**$6.95**
Josephine Roberts - Tanana	**$6.95**
Billy McCarty - Ruby	**$6.95**
Simeon Mountain - Nulato	**$8.95**
Altona Brown - Ruby	**$14.95**
The Darts - Manley Hot Springs	**$9.95**
Goodwin Semaken - Kaltag	**$9.95**
Henry Ekada - Nulato	**$7.95**
Stanley Dayo - Manley Hot Springs	**$10.95**
Peter John - Minto	**$7.95**

Coming Soon:
Martha Joe - Nulato

POSTAGE AND HANDLING
Add $1.00 for first book, 50ᶜ for each additional book. Orders of 10 or more, shipping will be billed.

Send order to:
Spirit Mountain Press
P.O. Box 1214   Fairbanks, Alaska 99707

Al Wright's Family Tree

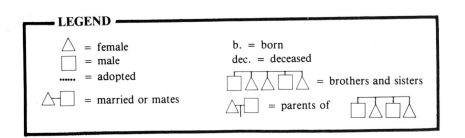

LEGEND

△ = female   b. = born

□ = male   dec. = deceased

..... = adopted   □△△□△ = brothers and sisters

△–□ = married or mates   △┬□ = parents of   □△□△

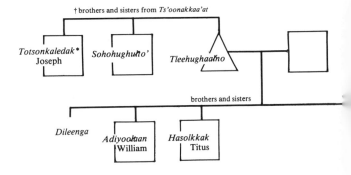

† brothers and sisters from *Ts'oonakkaa'at*

Totsonkaledak* Joseph   *Sohohughułto'*   *Tleehughaałno*

brothers and sisters

Dileenga   *Adiyoołaan* William   *Hasolkkak* Titus

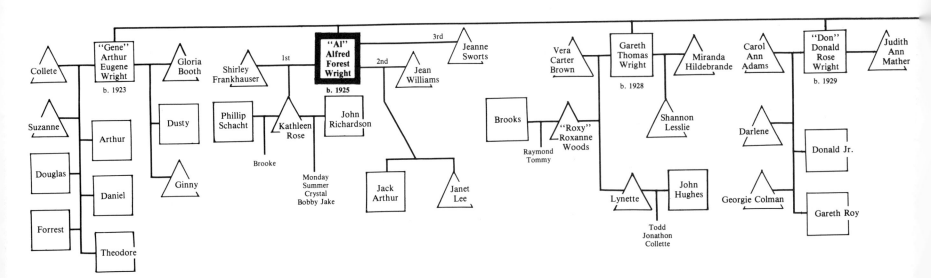

Collete — "Gene" Arthur Eugene Wright b. 1923 — Gloria Booth — Shirley Frankhauser — 1st — "Al" Alfred Forest Wright b. 1925 — 2nd — Jean Williams — 3rd — Jeanne Sworts

Suzanne — Arthur

Douglas

Forrest — Daniel — Theodore

Dusty — Ginny

Phillip Schacht — Kathleen Rose — John Richardson

Brooke

Monday Summer Crystal Bobby Jake

Jack Arthur — Janet Lee

Vera Carter Brown — Gareth Thomas Wright b. 1928 — Miranda Hildebrande

Brooks — "Roxy" Roxanne Woods

Raymond Tommy

Shannon Lesslie

Lynette — John Hughes

Todd Jonathon Collette

Carol Ann Adams — "Don" Donald Rose Wright b. 1929 — Judith Ann Mather

Darlene

Georgie Colman — Donald Jr. — Gareth Roy